AF258988

# Text

Read the verese and pay attention to anything that the Spirit highlights.

# Immerse

Study the highlighted verse or phrase, by using various Bible tools/software
so you can understand it more deeply. Record anything you learn.

# Ministry

Ask God how He wants to apply this to your life.
How does He want to transform you?
What action might He want you to take?

# Encounter

Take your learning and application to God in prayer.
Talk with God and listen to Him.
Close your time in worship and adoration.

The goal of this time is to enter into the presence of God laying your cares
before Him, being empowered by His Spirit, and worshiping Him for who He is.

**T.I.M.E. Bible Reading Method - Tyson, Jon; Silk, Suzy. Kingdom Values (Foundations Book 1) (p. 14).**

# Psalm 119
# New century Version

# vs. 1-8

1 Happy are those who live pure lives,
   who follow the Lord's teachings.

2 Happy are those who keep his rules,
   who try to obey him with their whole heart.

3 They don't do what is wrong:
   they follow his ways.

4 Lord, you gave your orders
   to be obeyed completely.

5 I wish I were more loyal
   in obeying your demands.

6 Then I would not be ashamed
   when I study your commands.

7 When I learned that your laws are fair,
   I praised you with an honest heart.

8 I will obey your demands,
   so please don't ever leave me.

vs.1

# vs. 9-16

9 How can a young person live a pure life?
   By obeying your word.

10 With all my heart I try to obey you.
   Don't let me break your commands.

11 I have taken your words to heart:
   so I would not sin against you.

12 Lord, you should be praised.
   Teach me your demands.

13 My lips will tell about
   all the laws you have spoken.

14 I enjoy living by your rules
   as people enjoy great riches.

15 I think about your orders
   and study your ways.

16 I enjoy obeying your demands.
   and I will not forget your word.

vs. 10

# vs. 17-24

17 Do good to me, your servant, so I can live,
   so I can obey your word.

18 Open my eyes to see
   the miracles in your teachings.

19 I am a stranger on earth.
   Do not hide your commands from me.

20 I wear myself out with desire
   for your laws all the time.

21 You scold proud people:
   those who ignore your commands are cursed.

22 Don't let me be insulted and hated
   because I keep your rules.

23 Even if princes speak against me,
   I, your servant, will think about your demands.

24 Your rules give me pleasure:
   they give me good advice.

vs. 20

# vs. 25-32

25 I am about to die.
   Give me life, as you have promised.

26 I told you about my life, and you answered me.
   Teach me your demands.

27 Help me understand your orders.
   Then I will think about your miracles.

28 I am sad and tired.
   Make me strong again as you have promised.

29 Don't let me be dishonest:
   have mercy on me by helping me obey your teachings.

30 I have chosen the way of truth:
   I have obeyed your laws.

31 I hold on to your rules.
   Lord, do not let me be disgraced.

32 I will quickly obey your commands,
   because you have made me happy.

vs. 32

# vs. 33-40

33 Lord, teach me your demands,
   and I will keep them until the end.

34 Help me understand, so I can keep your teachings,
   obeying them with all my heart.

35 Lead me in the path of your commands,
   because that makes me happy.

36 Make me want to keep your rules
   instead of wishing for riches.

37 Keep me from looking at worthless things.
   Let me live by your word.

38 Keep your promise to me, your servant,
   so you will be respected.

39 Take away the shame I fear,
   because your laws are good.

40 How I want to follow your orders.
   Give me life because of your goodness.

vs. 36

# vs. 41-48

41 Lord, show me your love,
   and save me as you have promised.

42 I have an answer for people who insult me,
   because I trust what you say.

43 Never keep me from speaking your truth,
   because I depend on your fair laws.

44 I will obey your teachings
   forever and ever.

45 So I will live in freedom,
   because I want to follow your orders.

46 I will discuss your rules with kings
   and will not be ashamed.

47 I enjoy obeying your commands,
   which I love.

48 I praise your commands, which I love,
   and I think about your demands.

vs. 48

# vs. 49-56

49 Remember your promise to me, your servant:
    it gives me hope.

50 When I suffer, this comforts me:
    Your promise gives me life.

51 Proud people always make fun of me,
    but I do not reject your teachings.

52 I remember your laws from long ago,
    and they comfort me, Lord.

53 I become angry with wicked people
    who do not keep your teachings.

54 I sing about your demands
    wherever I live.

55 Lord, I remember you at night,
    and I will obey your teachings.

56 This is what I do:
    I follow your orders.

vs. 54

# vs. 57-64

57 Lord, you are my share in life:
   I have promised to obey your words.

58 I prayed to you with all my heart.
   Have mercy on me as you have promised.

59 I thought about my life,
   and I decided to follow your rules.

60 I hurried and did not wait
   to obey your commands.

61 Wicked people have tied me up,
   but I have not forgotten your teachings.

62 In the middle of the night, I get up to thank you
   because your laws are right.

63 I am a friend to everyone who fears you,
   to anyone who obeys your orders.

64 Lord, your love fills the earth.
   Teach me your demands.

vs. 62

# vs. 65-72

65  You have done good things for your servant.□
    as you have promised. Lord.

66  Teach me wisdom and knowledge□
    because I trust your commands.

67  Before I suffered, I did wrong.□
    but now I obey your word.

68 You are good. and you do what is good.□
    Teach me your demands.

69 Proud people have made up lies about me.□
    but I will follow your orders with all my heart.

70  Those people have no feelings.□
    but I love your teachings.

71 It was good for me to suffer□
    so I would learn your demands.

72 Your teachings are worth more to me□
    than thousands of pieces of gold and silver.

vs.72

# vs. 73-80

73 You made me and formed me with your hands.
   Give me understanding so I can learn your commands.

74 Let those who respect you rejoice when they see me.
   because I put my hope in your word.

75 Lord, I know that your laws are right
   and that it was right for you to punish me.

76 Comfort me with your love.
   as you promised me. your servant.

77 Have mercy on me so that I may live.
   I love your teachings.

78 Make proud people ashamed because they lied about me.
   But I will think about your orders.

79 Let those who respect you return to me,
   those who know your rules.

80 Let me obey your demands perfectly
   so I will not be ashamed.

vs. 73

# vs. 81-88

81 I am weak from waiting for you to save me,
   but I hope in your word.

82 My eyes are tired from looking for your promise.
   When will you comfort me?

83 Even though I am like a wine bag going up in smoke,
   I do not forget your demands.

84 How long will I live?
   When will you judge those who are hurting me?

85 Proud people have dug pits to trap me.
   They have nothing to do with your teachings.

86 All of your commands can be trusted.
   Liars are hurting me. Help me!

87 They have almost put me in the grave,
   but I have not rejected your orders.

88 Give me life by your love
   so I can obey your rules.

vs. 82

# vs. 89-96

89 Lord, your word is everlasting;
   it continues forever in heaven.

90 Your loyalty will go on and on:
   you made the earth, and it still stands.

91 All things continue to this day because of your laws,
   because all things serve you.

92 If I had not loved your teachings,
   I would have died from my sufferings.

93 I will never forget your orders,
   because you have given me life by them.

94 I am yours. Save me,
   I want to obey your orders.

95 Wicked people are waiting to destroy me,
   but I will think about your rules.

96 Everything I see has its limits,
   but your commands have none.

vs. 90

# vs. 97-104

97 How I love your teachings!
    I think about them all day long.

98 Your commands make me wiser than my enemies,
    because they are mine forever.

99 I am wiser than all my teachers,
    because I think about your rules.

100 I have more understanding than the elders,
    because I follow your orders.

101 I have avoided every evil way
    so I could obey your word.

102 I haven't walked away from your laws,
    because you yourself are my teacher.

103 Your promises are sweet to me,
    sweeter than honey in my mouth!

104 Your orders give me understanding,
    so I hate lying ways.

vs. 103

# vs. 105-112

105 Your word is like a lamp for my feet
and a light for my path.

106 I will do what I have promised
and obey your fair laws.

107 I have suffered for a long time.
Lord, give me life by your word.

108 Lord, accept my willing praise
and teach me your laws.

109 My life is always in danger,
but I haven't forgotten your teachings.

110 Wicked people have set a trap for me,
but I haven't strayed from your orders.

111 I will follow your rules forever,
because they make me happy.

112 I will try to do what you demand
forever, until the end.

vs. 105

# vs. 113-120

113 I hate disloyal people,
    but I love your teachings.

114 You are my hiding place and my shield:
    I hope in your word.

115 Get away from me, you who do evil,
    so I can keep my God's commands.

116 Support me as you promised so I can live.
    Don't let me be embarrassed because of my hopes.

117 Help me, and I will be saved.
    I will always respect your demands.

118 You reject those who ignore your demands,
    because their lies mislead them.

119 You throw away the wicked of the world like trash.
    So I will love your rules.

120 I shake in fear of you:
    I respect your laws.

vs. 114

# vs. 121-128

121 I have done what is fair and right.
    Don't leave me to those who wrong me.

122 Promise that you will help me, your servant.
    Don't let proud people wrong me.

123 My eyes are tired from looking for your salvation
    and for your good promise.

124 Show your love to me, your servant,
    and teach me your demands.

125 I am your servant. Give me wisdom
    so I can understand your rules.

126 Lord, it is time for you to do something,
    because people have disobeyed your teachings.

127 I love your commands
    more than the purest gold.

128 I respect all your orders,
    so I hate lying ways.

vs.126

129 Your rules are wonderful.
That is why I keep them.

130 Learning your words gives wisdom
and understanding for the foolish.

131 I am nearly out of breath.
I really want to learn your commands.

132 Look at me and have mercy on me
as you do for those who love you.

133 Guide my steps as you promised;
don't let any sin control me.

134 Save me from harmful people
so I can obey your orders.

135 Show your kindness to me, your servant.
Teach me your demands.

136 Tears stream from my eyes,
because people do not obey your teachings.

vs. 136

# vs. 137-144

137 Lord, you do what is right,
   and your laws are fair.

138 The rules you commanded are right
   and completely trustworthy.

139 I am so upset I am worn out,
   because my enemies have forgotten your words.

140 Your promises are proven,
   so I, your servant, love them.

141 I am unimportant and hated,
   but I have not forgotten your orders.

142 Your goodness continues forever.
   and your teachings are true.

143 I have had troubles and misery,
   but I love your commands.

144 Your rules are always good.
   Help me understand so I can live.

vs. 142

# vs. 145-152

145 Lord, I call to you with all my heart.
Answer me, and I will keep your demands.

146 I call to you.
Save me so I can obey your rules.

147 I wake up early in the morning and cry out.
I hope in your word.

148 I stay awake all night
so I can think about your promises.

149 Listen to me because of your love:
Lord, give me life by your laws.

150 Those who love evil are near,
but they are far from your teachings.

151 But, Lord, you are also near,
and all your commands are true.

152 Long ago I learned from your rules
that you made them to continue forever.

vs. 147

# vs. 153-160

**153** See my suffering and rescue me,
   because I have not forgotten your teachings.

**154** Argue my case and save me.
   Let me live by your promises.

**155** Wicked people are far from being saved,
   because they do not want your demands.

**156** Lord, you are very kind:
   give me life by your laws.

**157** Many enemies are after me,
   but I have not rejected your rules.

**158** I see those traitors, and I hate them,
   because they do not obey what you say.

**159** See how I love your orders.
   Lord, give me life by your love.

**160** Your words are true from the start,
   and all your laws will be fair forever.

vs. 154

# vs. 161-168

161 Leaders attack me for no reason,
but I fear your law in my heart.

162 I am as happy over your promises
as if I had found a great treasure.

163 I hate and despise lies,
but I love your teachings.

164 Seven times a day I praise you
for your fair laws.

165 Those who love your teachings will find true peace,
and nothing will defeat them.

166 I am waiting for you to save me, Lord.
I will obey your commands.

167 I obey your rules,
and I love them very much.

168 I obey your orders and rules,
because you know everything I do.

vs. 165

# vs. 169-176

169 Hear my cry to you, Lord.
    Let your word help me understand.

170 Listen to my prayer:
    save me as you promised.

171 Let me speak your praise,
    because you have taught me your demands.

172 Let me sing about your promises,
    because all your commands are fair.

173 Give me your helping hand,
    because I have chosen your commands.

174 I want you to save me, Lord.
    I love your teachings.

175 Let me live so I can praise you,
    and let your laws help me.

176 I have wandered like a lost sheep.
    Look for your servant, because I have
    not forgotten your commands.

vs. 176

# STUDY
# RESOURCES

# Commentaries

www.enduringword.com

www.biblehub.com


# Bibles

www.biblegateway.com

www.bible.com

www.netbible.org


# Phone Apps

**You Version**

**Fighter Verses**


# Prayer App

**Echo Prayer**


# Bible Studies

**Messenger X App**

**Right Now Media** (If you need a login contact katie@newlifemi.com)

**Walking the Text** - walkingthetext.com